U.S. Army Rangers

by James Koons

Illustrated with photographs by Alan and
Frieda Landau/Blue Thunder Pictures

M I N N E A P O L I S

Printed in the United States of America.

Capstone Press • 2440 Fernbrook Lane • Minneapolis, MN 55447

Editorial Director   John Coughlan
Managing Editor   Tom Streissguth
Production Editor   James Stapleton
Book Design   Timothy Halldin

Library-of-Congress Cataloging-in-Publication Data

Koons, James, 1970--
     U.S. Army Rangers / by James Koons.
      p. cm. -- (Serving your country)
     Includes bibliographical references (p. 46) and index.
     Summary: Covers the history of the U.S. Army Rangers and the training required to be a member of this elite infantry corps.
     ISBN 1-56065-284-5
     1. United States. Army--Commando troops--Juvenile literature. [1. United States. Army--Commando troops.] I. Title. II. Series.
  UA34.R36K66 1996
  356'.167'0973--dc20   95-440
                                                          CIP
                                                          AC

Table of Contents

Chapter 1 Just a Few More Hours......................5

Chapter 2 The History of Army Rangers............9

Chapter 3 Vietnam, Iraq, and the 75th Ranger
Regiment.......................................17

Chapter 4 Ranger Training...............................21

Chapter 5 Operation Urgent Fury 33

Chapter 6 Becoming a Ranger 39

Chapter 7 Standing Orders, Rogers' Rangers ...41

Glossary 44

To Learn More 46

Some Useful Addresses 47

Index 48

Chapter 1

Just a Few More Hours

The time is 0500 (5 a.m.). The sky is still dark. The trainee has slept only four hours in the last eight days. His eyelids are heavy, and his stomach is empty.

His last meal came in a small foil package. It tasted like wet sawdust. He had to gulp it down in 10 minutes. Since coming to Ranger school nine weeks ago, he has lost 16 pounds (7.2 kilograms).

His patrol boat glides quietly down the river. A branch ahead shakes. The trainee looks at his

Members of the U.S. Army Rangers pose with weapons and in combat camouflage.

Using a rope, a Ranger trainee crosses a rushing river with a full pack.

buddy, then glances at the other four trainees on the boat. Did that branch really move?

Are the **opfors** (soldiers posing as the enemy) planning another ambush? The boat nears the branch. Something falls from it. The object plops into the black water and slips away. It's just a snake. It looks like the snake the trainee tasted at survival training.

In a few hours, the trainees will land on a beach. Others who have not yet dropped out will be with them. Together, they must use all the skills they have learned. If their mission succeeds, they will be Army Rangers.

What Rangers Do

Army Rangers are one of the world's best-trained fighting forces. In just 18 hours, they can be in any jungle or desert in the world. They get there by land, sea, or air. They can survive in the harshest wilderness for three or more days without resupply.

Army Rangers overcome all obstacles, no matter how difficult. Ranger school gives them the confidence to do it.

Chapter 2

The History of Army Rangers

The world's best soldiers were first called "Rangers" more than 200 years ago. Like today's Army Rangers, the first Rangers took on very dangerous missions. The regular army did not train its soldiers for such tasks.

Guerrilla Fighting

In 1754, a war broke out between Great Britain and France. These European countries were fighting for control of the rivers and lakes

Rangers set off on a cross-country run.

in the North American **colonies**. Native Americans fought for both armies in this French and Indian War (1754-1763).

British soldiers were used to fighting on large, open fields. They weren't ready for **guerrilla** warfare in the North American forests. Their heavy backpacks and bright red coats made this kind of fighting difficult.

But the French soldiers were experienced guerrillas. Native Americans taught them how to survive and fight in the wilderness. The British were no match for the French.

Rogers' Rangers

The British asked the people living in the North American colonies for help. Some colonists formed **companies** of Rangers. One of these companies was Rogers' Rangers. Its leader was a woodsman named Robert Rogers (1731-1795). The company's members took the name "Rangers" because they easily roamed, or "ranged," in the forests. They could also carry out **reconnaissance** (spy) missions on the French.

Rangers prepare for combat under tough conditions.

Rogers' Rangers carried only what they needed. Each man had dried food, a small canteen, and a blanket. For weapons, each had a knife, a short musket, and ammunition. Their brown and green clothes helped **camouflage** them. They even used ice skates to cross frozen rivers and lakes. (For a list of the Rangers' first "standing orders," turn to page 41.)

With the help of the Rangers, the British defeated the French.

Rangers of the 19th Century

During the Civil War (1861-1865), many Rangers fought for the North against the Confederate (Southern) Army. They destroyed miles of Confederate railroad tracks and raided the enemy's camps.

But the most famous Rangers of the time were the Texas Rangers. Volunteers formed the Texas Rangers in the 1820s. During the Mexican War (1846-1848), Texas Rangers were heroic scouts. Later, they were legendary lawmen. One of the most famous Texas Rangers was Pat Garrett (1850-1908).

In 1874, the Texas Rangers became an official law-enforcement agency. Unlike most Ranger groups, the Texas Rangers never split up. They are law enforcers to this day.

World War II

During World War II (1939-1945), the United States needed **commandos** for the fight against Germany. The U.S. Army formed a new unit and named it after the Rangers. For the

A squad of Ranger infantry recreates a World War II Ranger battle in a mock village.

first time, Rangers were official members of the United States Army.

There were six Ranger **battalions** in World War II. The 1st, 3rd, and 4th battalions fought in Italy and North Africa. During Operation Torch, the 1st Rangers went ashore in North Africa before the regular Army. The Rangers destroyed enemy defenses. They cleared the beach for a larger invasion by other U.S. forces.

The 1st, 3rd, and 4th battalions also invaded Sicily and Italy. They destroyed enemy defenses and captured enemy prisoners. Tough and experienced, the Rangers were able to capture the town of Salerno in just a few hours.

Korean War

After World War II, the Ranger units disbanded. But in the early 1950s, the United States was at war again. This time, U.S. forces

This North Korean flag was captured by the 8th Ranger Company during the Korean War.

were defending South Korea from North Korean and Chinese attacks. The army formed Ranger units early in the Korean War (1950-1953).

The Rangers who fought in Korea trained for 10 weeks. Training lasted more than 60 hours each week. The last four weeks of training were in the Colorado mountains. There, Rangers learned survival skills they would need for the cold Korean winters.

The Rangers were very successful in Korea. But after the war they were again disbanded. Many military leaders thought it was too expensive to train them. Others worried that Ranger units were taking good soldiers from regular units.

But Ranger units would soon prove their worth again.

Chapter 3

Vietnam, Iraq, and the 75th Ranger Regiment

During the Vietnam War (1954-1975), the U.S. Army formed several **Long Range Reconnaissance Patrols (LRRPs)**. LRRPs were called Rangers for short. They performed the same kinds of missions as the Rangers did in World War II and Korea.

Most Ranger missions in Vietnam lasted a week. The Rangers got very little sleep and carried all their equipment on their backs. This was very difficult in Vietnam's hot and humid jungles.

A Long Range Surveillance Unit, made up of skilled Ranger fighters, leaps from a Blackhawk helicopter.

The U.S. Army wanted to form small, expert units that could travel halfway around the world in 18 hours. In 1974, the army formed two permanent Ranger battalions. The 1st Battalion trained at Fort Benning, Georgia. The 2nd Battalion trained at Fort Lewis, Washington.

In 1983, the Rangers took part in Operation Urgent Fury on the island of Grenada. Pleased with the success of the mission, the army added the 3rd Ranger Battalion. In 1987, the three battalions combined to form the 75th Ranger Regiment.

Operation Desert Storm

In Operation Desert Storm in 1991, the Rangers trained regular army units for reconnaissance missions in Iraq. The training allowed soldiers to sneak behind enemy lines and stay under cover. Although the enemy came as close as 10 feet (3 meters), they could not spot the hidden U.S. troops.

After Iraq was defeated, the Rangers held a short exercise. They parachuted into the country in broad daylight. The jump served as a warning. It reminded the Iraqi leaders of the skills and training of these elite units.

Chapter 4
Ranger Training

Each year, 3,000 men enter Ranger school. The grueling training takes 68 days, and trainees must be in excellent physical condition. Once a soldier becomes a Ranger, he continues to train five days a week and 48 weeks a year.

Ranger school includes four phases, each of which takes place at different camps. Each camp is in a different environment, from hot and dry deserts to cold mountaintops.

A Ranger prepares for a drop into water during the Best Ranger competition.

Push-ups and other physical training are a daily part of Ranger training.

Ranger training is as much like real combat as possible. Students sleep only about three hours a day. Rarely do they get more than one or two meals a day. Often, their food comes in cold **MREs (meals ready to eat)**. The lack of food and sleep makes judgment difficult. By the end of training, students are using their instincts and the skills they have learned to survive.

The lack of sleep and food, and the hard physical exercise, make Ranger training very tough. But Rangers believe the hardships are worth it. This is the only way to earn the black-and-gold Ranger **insignia**. The insignia proves they are members of the most famous fighting force in the world.

Fort Benning, Georgia

Trainees begin with the 4th Training Brigade at Fort Benning, Georgia. Those with parachute experience jump into camp. Others arrive by truck.

During the busy first day, trainees must pass the army's physical test. The test includes 52 push-ups, 62 sit-ups, six chin-ups, and a two-mile (3.2-kilometer) run. The run must be completed in less than 14 minutes. Most trainees pass this test with little trouble.

Next, they take a combat water survival test. There is a 15-meter (49.5-foot) swim in full combat gear. Trainees must submerge themselves underwater and discard the gear. Finally, they walk off a diving board blindfolded. While underwater, they must remove the blindfold and swim to poolside without losing any gear. If the trainees show any fear during the water tests, they fail.

On the first day, trainees are assigned buddies who will remain with them during training. Many buddies remain good friends throughout the training and for the rest of their lives.

The Ranger Stakes

On the second day, students take the **Ranger Stakes**. The stakes are 11 quick tests. Trainees must pass seven of the tests to move on. Those who fail are trained and retested immediately. If a trainee fails a second time, he must start training all over again when the next class arrives. The stakes test knowledge of weaponry and of radio communications.

Rangers must prepare for operations on land, in the air, and through the water.

Hard Training

Each day at Fort Benning begins with a five-mile (eight-kilometer) run. Another difficult physical test is the confidence course. First, trainees climb a 13-foot (3.9-meter) log fence without ropes. Next, they crawl through the famous worm pit. The worm pit is 82 feet (24.6 meters) of mud covered by knee-high barbed wire. While trainees crawl beneath the barbed wire, instructors keep the mud wet with hoses.

After the worm pit, trainees cross another mud pit on slippery rafters 32 feet (9.6 meters)

Trainees practice hand-to-hand combat techniques.

above the pit. If they fall, they must begin over. Finally, they must crawl up a high rope net and slide down another rope.

The rest of the time at Fort Benning is spent learning combat skills. Each evening, trainees practice hand-to-hand combat for three or four hours. In a classroom, they learn patrolling and leadership.

Trainees also learn how to catch and cook small animals. That day, they may eat only once. This way, instructors can be sure the students will have their "Ranger stew."

Fort Bliss, Texas

On the 16th day, trainees fly to the 7th Training Brigade at Fort Bliss, Texas. Here they learn desert combat and survival skills.

During **field exercises**, they carry out ambush and reconnaissance missions. Some instructors pose as enemy forces. These "enemies" are called opfors. Often, opfors use real enemy weapons and uniforms. Opfors even have prisoner-of-war camps. "Captured" students are treated as much like prisoners of war as possible.

The trainees get only one or two hours of sleep a night. They eat only one MRE a day. After training at Fort Bliss, usually only 60 percent of the original class is left. Some students fail. Others are injured or become ill. If they choose, they may start over when the next class arrives.

Dahlonega, Georgia

On the 34th day, trainees take a bus to Dahlonega, Georgia. There, they begin mountain training with the 5th Training Brigade. The first few days are spent learning knots and **rappelling**. Students learn to rappel a 60-foot (18-meter) cliff while carrying a buddy. To pass, they must also rappel the cliff while only touching it twice. Finally, they learn to rappel with a full backpack.

Students also learn important mountain climbing skills. They learn to climb and

Rangers advance under cover of smoke grenades.

descend, and how to transport heavy equipment up a mountainside.

Camp Rudder, Florida

The final phase takes place at Camp Rudder, Florida, where the 6th Training Brigade teaches jungle skills.

Many consider Camp Rudder the toughest phase of Ranger school. It is swampy, damp, and hot. Trainees who are still in the program are exhausted. Some start having **hallucinations**. Even trainees who make it through Camp Rudder sometimes quit. They decide the Rangers are not for them.

By the time they reach Camp Rudder, they have mastered reconnaissance and patrol methods. They now learn advanced techniques, such as advancing while under enemy fire.

At Camp Rudder, students also take a reptile class. They learn about snakes and alligators, and they also learn first aid for snakebites. To help the class, the army keeps a snake house and an alligator pond at the camp.

At Camp Rudder, students also learn to handle small boats. They cross streams and paddle to patrol bases marked on maps.

The field exercises are the hardest of the entire Ranger school. For nine days, trainees use their new skills in the swamps. They rarely

The Ranger competition includes a difficult canoe event.

sleep. Judgment is extremely difficult, and many students become confused.

On the 69th day, the remaining students return to Fort Benning. There, they have a huge meal and a full night's sleep. But to graduate, students must pass half of their field exercises and evaluations by their peers. They must also pass a leadership evaluation.

Less than 30 percent of graduates finish Ranger school with the class they began with. Of the 3,000 who enter the school each year, less than half will ever earn the Ranger insignia.

Chapter 5

Operation Urgent Fury

In 1983, the Soviet Union and Cuba began to build military bases on Grenada, a small island in the Caribbean Sea. The United States government believed that an unfriendly military there would pose a threat. The U. S. quickly planned an invasion.

The military planned to capture an enemy airfield and to rescue American medical students on the island. The 1st and 2nd Ranger

A Ranger rappels down a steep cliff.

battalions were chosen to head Operation Urgent Fury.

The Rangers had little time to prepare. Just a few hours after receiving orders, they were aboard airplanes at Hunter Army Airfield in Alabama.

Some parts of the mission didn't go as planned. The Rangers prepared to land Company A and Company C at the airfield before dawn. But a Navy reconnaissance team could not get ashore to gather information for

the Rangers. Nevertheless, as dawn broke, the Rangers decided to go ahead with the mission.

On October 25 at 0536 (5:36 a.m.), Rangers from A Company began their jump over Grenada. After landing, they met at the eastern edge of the airfield. They learned C Company had been sent elsewhere. This meant A Company would have to perform its mission alone.

The Cubans left many vehicles parked on the airfield. The Rangers moved the vehicles and used a Cuban bulldozer to knock over fences. After a brisk gun battle with the Cubans, the Rangers took over the airfield. By 0700 (7:00 a.m.), the 1st Battalion was in control.

At that same time, the 2nd Battalion arrived. They parachuted onto the western edge of the airfield. Once there, they secured the area. Members of the 1st Battalion moved onto the medical school. At 0850 (8:50 a.m.), the campus was secure. The Rangers accomplished

Trainees hit the beach during a landing operation.

their main goals on the first day of the
operation.

After a few more days, the Rangers flew
back to the United States. The success of the

mission prompted the military to form the 3rd Ranger Battalion.

The Rangers' bravery was not without a cost. In Operation Urgent Fury, five Rangers were killed and six others wounded.

The Rangers overcame many obstacles, but they remembered their training. They had already passed one of the most difficult schools in the world.

Invasion plans sometimes call for Rangers to jump into battle.

Chapter 6

Becoming a Ranger

The goal of the Ranger school is to produce excellent leaders. All male officers and non-commissioned officers (NCOs) are eligible to apply for Ranger school. Such men already have leadership experience. Soldiers of lower rank may also apply. First, they need permission from their commanders.

Men from all branches of the U.S. armed forces may volunteer. Most Rangers are from the U.S. Army. A few come from the navy, air force, or marines. Although most Rangers are American, soldiers from other armed forces **allied** with the United States may also apply. But there are very few foreign soldiers in Ranger school.

Chapter 7

Standing Orders, Rogers' Rangers

1. Don't forget anything.

2. Have your musket clean as a whistle, hatchet scoured, sixty rounds powder and ball, and be ready to march at a minute's warning.

3. When you're on the march, act the way you would if you were sneaking up on a deer. See the enemy first.

4. Tell the truth about what you see and what you do. You can lie all you please when you tell other folks about the Rangers, but don't ever lie to a Ranger or to an officer.

5. Don't take any unnecessary chances.

6. When we're on the march we march single file, far enough apart so one shot won't go through two men.

7. If we strike swamps, or soft ground, we spread out abreast, so it's hard to track us.

8. When we march, we keep moving till dark, so as to give the enemy the least chance at us.

9. When we camp, half the party stays awake while the other half sleeps.

10. If we take prisoners, we keep them separate until we have had enough time to examine them, so they can't cook up a story between them.

11. Never march home the same way. Take a different route so you won't be ambushed.

12. No matter whether we travel in big parties or little ones, each party has to keep a scout 20 yards ahead, 20 yards on each flank, and 20 yards in the rear, so the main body can't be surprised and wiped out.

13. Each night you'll be told where to meet if surrounded by a superior force.

14. Don't sit down to eat without posting sentries.

15. Don't sleep beyond dawn.

16. Don't cross a river by a regular ford.

17. If somebody's trailing you, make a circle, come back onto your own tracks, and ambush the folks that aim to ambush you.

18. Don't stand up when the enemy's coming against you. Kneel down or lie down.

19. Let the enemy come till he's almost close enough to touch. Then let him have it and jump out and finish him up with your hatchet.

--Major Robert Rogers, 1759

The official Ranger flash shield.

Glossary

allied–the name given to countries which are friendly to the United States

battalion–a military unit made up of as many as 500 soldiers

colonies–areas settled by people from foreign countries

commando–a soldier trained to perform dangerous missions

company–a group of about 150 soldiers

field exercises–practices at Ranger school that simulate real combat situations

guerrilla–a member of a small fighting force that operates behind enemy lines.

hallucinations–visions of objects that aren't present. Hallucinations can be caused by hard training and fatigue.

insignia–a symbol of membership in a group

Long Range Reconnaissance Patrols (LRRPs)–small groups of U.S. commandos who performed reconnaissance and demolition missions in Vietnam

MREs (meals ready to eat)–small packages of food eaten by soldiers in the field

opfors–name given to U.S. soldiers who pose as enemies during field exercises

Ranger Stakes–one of the first series of tests hopeful Rangers face at Ranger school

rappelling–using a rope to descend a cliff

reconnaissance–a military mission designed to get information about the enemy

To Learn More

Eyewitness Visual Dictionary Series. *Special Military Forces.* New York: Dorling Kindersley, Inc. 1993.

Landau, Alan M. and Frieda W. *Army Rangers.* Osceola, WI: Motorbooks International, 1992.

Miller, David. *Modern Elite Forces.* New York: Smithmark Publishers, 1992.

Paradis, Adrian A. *Opportunities in Military Careers.* Lincolnwood, IL: VGM Career Horizons, 1989.

U.S. Army Staff. *Ranger Handbook.* Boulder, CO: Paladin Press, 1993.

Some Useful Addresses

United States Army Infantry Center
Fort Benning, Georgia, 31905

Ranger Memorial Foundation
c/o NCOA Service Center
2029 S. Lumpkin Rd.
Columbus, GA 31903

Index

buddies, 6, 24

Camp Rudder, Florida, 29-30
Civil War, 12
commandos, 12
confidence course, 25-27

field exercises, 27, 30, 31
Fort Benning, Georgia, 18, 23, 25-27, 31
Fort Bliss, Texas, 27-28
Fort Lewis, Washington, 18
French and Indian War, 9-11

Garrett, Pat, 12
Grenada, 19, 33-35

insignia, 23, 35
Iraq, 19

Korean War, 14-15

Long Range Reconnaissance Patrols (LRRPs), 17

Mexican War, 12
meals ready-to-eat (MREs), 22, 28, 32
Native Americans, 10

Operation Desert Storm, 19
Operation Torch, 13
Operation Urgent Fury, 19, 33-37
opfors, 6, 27, 31

parachute, 19, 23, 35

Ranger Stakes, 24
Ranger stew, 27
rappelling, 28
reconnaissance missions, 10, 17, 19, 27, 30, 34
reptile class, 30
Rogers' Rangers, 10-11

Texas Rangers, 12

Vietnam War, 17

water survival test, 23
World War II, 12-14, 17
worm pit, 26